D1568575

!

Welcome to your Walking Stick Press guided
journal. Within these pages you'll find:

#

instruction to guide you on your way

#

writing prompts to lead you to your goal

#

blank pages to record your responses to the
prompts—to map your insights as you vent, heal,
and explore

#

quotes to inspire, provoke, and refresh you

#

Along the way, feel free to jot in the margins,
add your own quotes,
let writing take you down a trail you didn't expect.
Enjoy the journey.

#

THINGS THAT TICK ME OFF
!
a guided journal

Joan Mazza

Walking Stick Press
Cincinnati, Ohio

Things That Tick Me Off: A Guided Journal. Copyright © 2001 by Joan Mazza. Manufactured in the United States of America. All rights reserved. No part of this book may be reproduced in any form or by any electronic or mechanical means including information storage and retrieval systems without permission in writing from the publisher, except by a reviewer, who may quote brief passages in a review. Published by Walking Stick Press, an imprint of F&W Publications, Inc., 1507 Dana Avenue, Cincinnati, Ohio 45207. (800) 289-0963. First edition.

Visit our Web site at www.writersdigest.com for information on more resources for writers.

To receive a free weekly e-mail newsletter delivering tips and updates about writing and about Writer's Digest products, send an e-mail with "Subscribe Newsletter" in the body of the message to newsletter-request@writersdigest.com, or register directly at our Web site at www.writersdigest.com.

05 04 03 02 01   5 4 3 2 1

Library of Congress Cataloging-in-Publication Data

Mazza, Joan.
   Things that tick me off : a guided journal / by Joan Mazza.
      p. cm.
   Includes biographical references.
   ISBN 1-58297-020-3 (alk. paper)
      1. Anger. 2. Diaries—Authorship. I. Title.

BF575.A5 .M35 2000
152.4'7 21; aa05 07-28—dc00

                                                                00-043644

Edited by Michelle Howry and Jessica Yerega
Designed by Matthew Gaynor
Cover photography by Scott Cunningham, © Tony Stone Images
Production coordinated by Mark Griffin

DEDICATION

In memory of my mother,
Mary Cacciatore

ACKNOWLEDGMENTS

My thanks to ...

My friends who generously offered to read the manuscript in progress—Valerie Renwick-Porter, Lana Schulman, Mel Standen, Joyce Sweeney, and Noreen Wald.

My fellow authors and members of ASJA (American Society of Journalists and Authors) who contributed their thoughts and strategies for dealing with anger—Barbara Blossom Ashmun, Anita Bartholomew, Pat McNees, Sharon Naylor, Susan K. Perry, Sue Russell, Daylle Deanna Schwartz, and Gini Graham Scott.

Participants of the Twin Oaks e-mail OneList who contributed ideas and comments and had a very stimulating discussion about anger, conflict resolution, and promoting peace in community.

All my fellow authors in Joyce Sweeney's Thursday night writing group who continue to critique my work and show me how to improve my writing.

My energetic and very smart agent, Lori Perkins.

And to Michelle Howry and Jack Heffron at Walking Stick Press for their enthusiasm, support, suggestions, corrections, and ideas to make this a better book.

Life consists of a lot of minor annoyances and
a few matters of real consequence.
Harvey Penick

ABOUT THE AUTHOR

Joan Mazza, M.S. LMHC, is the author of *Dreaming Your Real Self: A Personal Approach to Dream Interpretation* (Perigee, 1998), *Who's Crazy, Anyway?* (iUniverse, 2000), *Dream Back Your Life: Taking Dream Messages Into Life Action* (Perigee, 2000), *From Dreams to Discovery* (Walking Stick Press, 2001) and a columnist for *Personal Journaling* magazine. She is a psychotherapist and licensed mental health counselor with a M.S. in counseling psychology. She conducts ongoing groups in South Florida as well as national seminars on a variety of topics including:

Journal Writing and Creativity
Journal Writing as Self-Therapy
Understanding Dreams and Nightmares
How to Say No With a Smile: Setting Personal
    Boundaries
When Life Gives You Lemons ...
Creating Personal Rituals and Ceremonies
Knowing Your Shadow and Subpersonalities
Conscious Sexuality
Motivate Yourself!
Malleable Minds

As a speaker, Joan Mazza brings seminars to both professionals and the public, addressing the concerns and frustrations of people in "mid-life" crises regardless of age. With humor and personal anecdotes, she invites people to be themselves, take risks, and dream back their lives.

She is a past-president of The Book Group of South Florida, an organization of authors and book industry professionals. Her short stories, articles, poetry, and essays have appeared in many publications, including *Playgirl, Personal Journaling,* and *Möbius.*

Check out her Web site at **www.joanmazza.com**

Table of Contents

part I **UNDERSTANDING ANGER**

chapter 1

HOW TO USE THIS BOOK

In the beginning, the universe was created. This made a lot of people very angry, and has been widely regarded as a bad idea.

Douglas Adams

We all get angry at times—about things that are out of our control, with the frustrations of everyday living, and toward the people we live and work with. The people we get most angry with are often those we love the most. Mouthing off in our journals is a way to let off steam and look beyond our anger to find a new perspective. Journaling about what ticks us off can help us discover compassion for what others do as well as compassion for ourselves and our reactions to others.

This book grew out of the understanding that many people who keep a personal journal use it to complain, groan, moan, and mouth off about what ticks them off. The ideas and writing prompts in this book will offer you new ways to explore what is behind your anger. You will learn how both expressing and not expressing anger can hurt or help you. By using the writing prompts, you will find what works best for you.

So why not just get angry and let your emotions

...holding in your reactions and beliefs or not expressing your feelings can also be damaging to your sense of self.

out? Studies show that people who regularly express their anger in words and actions—even without becoming overtly violent—are at greater risk for heart disease, high blood pressure, and the emotional letdowns that come in the wake of unbridled rage.

At the same time, holding in your reactions and beliefs or not expressing your feelings can also be damaging to your sense of self. It deceives others about who you are. For some, persistently hiding true feelings can lead to depression and physical symptoms. How you express your feelings seems to be the important factor.

This book gives you a place to express your anger safely. You'll explore your feelings in a controlled way that won't fuel your rage or encourage you to attack anyone else—verbally or physically. In many ways, the writing prompts are designed to help you clarify what makes you angry—to be reflective about your anger. Writing your answers to the prompts will give you other ways to think about all those things that tick you off. Without blasting off or exploding, you can let your anger out safely and thoughtfully, while simultaneously keeping the worst of it to yourself—in the pages of this journal.

To make the best use of this book, it will be helpful for you to understand your attitude and reactions toward anger—both your own anger and the anger of others. However you arrived at your beliefs and anger style, they're yours now—to change as you see fit or to live with as is. *Part I: Understanding Anger* will give you a chance to examine your anger style, your beliefs about anger and its consequences, and how you got to be where you are.

If you've spent your life holding in your anger, *Part II: What Makes You Angry* contains safe and fun suggestions of ways to ventilate your anger without overindulging in it. If, on the other hand, you acknowledge that you have a quick temper and are often sorry for what you say and do in explosions of anger, you might want to spend less time on Part II (you may already ventilate too well!) and spend more time on *Part III: Transforming and Using Anger Productively.*

Part III offers strategies to examine your thinking to see how it provokes or fuels your anger. These chapters also present techniques to refocus your thoughts and energy away from pure anger and into productive action. You can learn to take the surge of energy that comes with anger and turn it into action to address what is bothering you. Some examples of taking productive action are: changing the way you interpret the situation that makes you angry; asking someone else to change his or her behavior; or acting to make a change in the world through writing letters, lobbying, or starting an activist organization.

All three parts of this book will help you find the balance that is right for you when something ticks you off.

To make the best use of this book, it will be helpful for you to understand your attitude and reactions toward anger—both your own anger and the anger of others.

ABOUT THE WRITING PROMPTS

If you get to a writing prompt and don't know what to write, move on to the next one. Some questions will be more helpful to you than others. You can always come back to those you skipped.

!

Prompts

Choose the prompts that interest you most, and use the blank pages that follow to record your responses.

1. Remember a time when you were very young and felt angry. What happened?

2. When you were growing up, what were you told about being angry?

3. When you were growing up, what were you told about expressing anger?

4. Who first taught you this distinction between feeling anger and expressing it?

5. How did your parents (or parental figures) manage their anger? How did they show their anger toward you as a child?

6. What beliefs do you hold about your own anger?

7. Does your anger create other feelings in you? (For example, are you afraid, proud, or ashamed of your anger?)

8. When you are angry with yourself, what do you do? What do you say to yourself? What do you say about yourself to others?

9. When you are angry with others, what do you do? What do you say to them? If you don't say anything, what do you think of them?

10. What do you think and feel about yourself when you are angry with someone else?

11. How is your anger at home different from your anger in the workplace? (For example, you may shout at your spouse, but you can control yourself when you are tempted to shout at your boss.)

12. Ask a trusted friend what you're like when you're angry. Take notes.

13. Would you like to be able to express anger more or less often than you do now? Explain.

14. Have you ever damaged property when you were angry? Describe.

15. Have you ever hurt a relationship with your anger? Describe.

16. What other changes, if any, would you like to make in the way you manage your anger?

17. Do you believe anger is related to being authentic, honest, or real? How?

18. How can you be more authentic without simultaneously being angrier?

14 | *Don't be afraid to feel as angry or as loving as you can, because when you feel nothing, it's just death.*

Lena Horne

16 | *Anger is a brief lunacy.*

Horace

chapter 2

WHAT IS ANGER?

*Anger and jealousy can no
more bear to lose sight of
their objects than love.*

George Eliot

When we talk about what ticks us off, we have already begun to acknowledge our anger. But what is it? How do you know you're ticked off? What is anger to you?

Anger is an emotion, a physiological change in the body, and the many thoughts that may accompany these combined feelings. Some people, when very angry, are unable to think at all. Faced with strong emotions, their brains seem to turn to mush; their minds go blank. In some people, anger creates physical pain and tension that might lead to an upset stomach, headache, or blurred vision. You may experience anger as heat or confusion. Perhaps the word *anger* immediately triggers memories or other emotions such as fear and sadness.

Knowing how your body responds to anger can help you understand it and deal with it more effectively.

THEORIES OF ANGER
Blowing off steam

There are various theories of anger, many of them referring to anger as a force of energy in the body, with the power to build up to dangerous levels if it isn't released. Some authors say that, like a pressure cooker, we need to have a valve to "let off steam," or we will blow up. John Lee, in *Facing the Fire: Experiencing and Expressing Anger Appropriately*, calls this "safely losing control." "Anger is an energy in your body that needs to come out," he says. "You will feel better—'Ahhh!'—when you've expressed your anger."

Keeping a lid on

Other authors, notably Carol Tavris in *Anger: The Misunderstood Emotion*, caution against blowing off steam. According to her theory, expressing your anger without careful consideration can make you and others uncomfortable … or worse. "If your expressed rage causes another person to shoot you, it won't matter that you die with healthy arteries," Tarvis says. And even if the target of your anger doesn't shoot you or fire you from your job, your raging fit might leave you feeling embarrassed, ashamed, and remorseful. You may have a new set of problems in the rift you've created in this relationship. Talking about angry feelings or acting them out sometimes fuels anger and aggression rather than diminishing it.

So which theory is right?

Everyone is different. To say that all anger needs an outlet or, conversely, that expressing anger always makes you feel worse is dogmatic. It doesn't allow for individual differences and special circumstances that need to be taken into account when deciding what to do with your anger.

Ventilating your anger doesn't necessarily mean "letting someone have it." It can simply be putting your

By taking action on our anger, we could be sure that descendents were left to pass on our genes into subsequent generations.

thoughts and feelings into words—in a journal or with a trusted confidante who is not the target of your anger. Many studies show that talking about problems or strong feelings can improve both your mood and your health.

Getting angry is normal. In many ways, our anger is a signal that something is wrong. From an evolutionary perspective, our anger is still with us because it has, at least in some respects, served our species well. (On the other hand, it also has contributed to killing off millions of our species.) In the social organizations of early humans (tribes or clans), our anger alerted us to the urgency to protect our territory and our food against outsiders, as well as to defend our families. By taking action on our anger, we could be sure that descendents were left to pass our genes on to subsequent generations. But in our prehistoric ancestry, it's quite possible that those with the most unbridled anger didn't live to reproduce or protect their children.

For quick-tempered people, learning how to contain and reduce anger would be most helpful. For those who simmer, sulk, and feel victimized when they are unable to speak for themselves, some expression of anger might be helpful in resolving what makes them angry. You may choose to express your anger in your journal or to use your examination of your anger as preparation for discussion and negotiation with another person.

SOURCES OF ANGER

Internal anger

Anger may be internal or external. *Internal anger* is being angry with yourself, maybe because you believe you've done something stupid. You may feel like a jerk for repeatedly falling for the same old tricks. While you may also be angry with the person who made a fool of you, you really think you should have known better.

Internal anger may be based on what you did or didn't do. Or, you might be angry with yourself because you are in the middle of an inner conflict—having an argument with yourself about the choices you face when making an important decision.

Regrets. We can all look back over our lives—even over yesterday—and think about the things we did, but wish we hadn't done. We begin sentences with, "If only...." Had we known what we know now, we would have done things differently. Now we may become angry with ourselves. These may be recent regrets or those of long standing. For some people, this kind of remorse leads to a low-level, constant anger at themselves that saps their energy. Bringing these sorrows and disappointments into your consciousness means you can do something about them to make a change. Equally valid is our decision to not do anything. You can simply let your anger go.

Inner conflict. If you're arguing with yourself, feeling pulled between two or more choices, you might try clarifying which parts of you are in conflict. Maybe your inner spender is fighting with your inner tightwad. Or the part of you that is concerned about nutrition and exercise argues with the part of you that wants to loll in a hammock and eat cookies. We often see these inner arguments as a choice between X and Y, but they are often more complex than that. Seeing more choices can help us stop arguing with ourselves.

Recurring mistakes. When we make a mistake that we've made before, we may become very angry with ourselves. "What will it take for me to learn this lesson?" we ask. If we can see these mistakes as part of our learning curve, we are more likely to learn from them and stop re-

Bringing these sorrows and disappointments into your consciousness means you can do something about them to make a change.

peating them—instead of getting angry with ourselves. The anger can become a catalyst for a change in our behavior.

Procrastination. Discovering our own procrastination makes us very angry with ourselves, especially when we enter midlife and realize all that we've put off and may now never accomplish. As we get older, we are more aware of how little time we have. One of the ways I motivate myself to get things done—especially a big project like writing a book—is to remind myself how angry I will be with myself when I'm in my eighties and realize that I no longer have the time to write all the books I wanted to write.

Angry dreams and fantasies. Many people learn about their anger from their dreams and fantasies. Whether you are the angry person in the dream or you dream that someone else's anger is directed toward you, you might look at both as indications of your own unrecognized anger. If you fear examining your anger, you might get a better glimpse at it in your dreams. See my previous books for more information on dreams: *From Dreams to Discovery* (Walking Stick Press, 2001), *Dreaming Your Real Self: A Personal Approach to Dream Interpretation* (Perigee, 1998), and *Dream Back Your Life: Transforming Dreams Into Life Action—A Practical Guide to Dreams, Daydreams, and Fantasies* (Perigee, 2000).

External anger

We can be angry at many things in our lives outside of ourselves, as we'll explore in detail in Part II of this book. Let's look at the broadest category of external anger now.

Expectations in today's world. Each of us is born into a family, country, social class, and political era. We are so-

> If you fear examining your anger, you might get a better glimpse at it in your dreams.

cialized to behave in a certain way. Depending on where and when we live, we may be taught that it is impolite to show our faces or the bottoms of our feet, to speak in public, or to talk about our emotions. No matter how well we acclimate to the political and social winds of our time, these social expectations may still make us angry.

Similarly, we may feel that our era and place require that we have certain achievements to be considered a success. We may feel that we are expected to achieve a certain level of education, acquire property and financial security, marry, or have a minimum number of children to feel that we've made a success of our lives. These expectations may not be in keeping with our own personal goals or values, and so they tick us off!

We may also feel that we have to behave or look a certain way to be loved and accepted. For example, many of us have been told (and still are told by the fashion magazines and experts) how we should look. If we feel we can't be authentic or honest, that is likely to make us angry, too.

> We may feel we have to behave or look a certain way to be loved or accepted.

Prompts

Choose the prompts that interest you most, and use the blank pages that follow to record your responses.

1. Quickly fill in the blanks below, and see what you say about anger. Don't think about the correct or technical answer. This is a journal, and everything you write is correct for you in the moment you write it.

Anger is _____

Anger is _____

Anger is _____

Anger is _____

Anger is _____

2. Describe your anger using the following prompts. Does anger have:
   # Color(s)?
   # Form?
   # Shape?
   # Sound?
   # Smell?
   # Taste?
   # Ideas?
   # Action or movement?
   # Particular words or thoughts?

3. How do you know when you're angry?

4. Where is anger felt or stored in your body?

5. How do you feel when you are angry?

6. What do your answers tell you about yourself?

7. Do you subscribe to the theory that people need to "let off steam" occasionally? If not, how do you refute it?

8. When you "pop off," how do you feel afterward?

9. Do you think you need to learn to keep anger in or let it out? How? What gives you the best results?

10. When is your anger justified? When is your anger helpful?

11. When does your anger signal you to act in a way that is good for you?

12. How can you use your anger as positive energy?

13. How do you regulate your anger?

14. How do you defuse others when they are angry?

We praise a man who feels
angry on the right grounds
and against the right
persons and also in the
right manner at the right
moment and for the right
length of time.

Aristotle

*Anger and intolerance are
the twin enemies of correct
understanding.*

Mahatma Gandhi

chapter 3

WHAT SHOULD YOU DO WITH ANGER?

The writing prompts at the end of chapter one offered a beginning for examining the way you deal with anger. Obviously, what you may do, think, say, or feel about your anger will be different depending on the specific situation.

Before diving into this journal, you have had your own ways to deal with your anger. Whether you have stifled, ignored, denied, accepted or expressed it, your approach has probably become automatic. To begin, let's examine your anger style.

THE MANY FACES OF ANGER

Anger can surface in many ways. When expressed indirectly, anger might come out as being contrary or difficult; when expressed directly, it may be a full-blown tantrum. These forms are common among children, but some adults also show anger in these ways. They might disagree with everything said by others—or by particular others such as spouses, parents, and children. Or they might pitch fits over small offenses.

Other faces of anger include depression, withdrawal, martyrdom, procrastination, and "forgetting." For example, adolescents are well known for sullen withdrawal when they don't get their way, but most of us can name adults who do the same. They withdraw to their rooms or some other private space to be alone and think of themselves as a victim of mistreatment. In such a situation, being angry might be appropriate and justified, but the method of expression doesn't make these people feel better, nor does it solve the problem.

Similarly, being contemptuous or critical of others can be an expression of anger. We say those people are "stupid assholes," and we might go so far as to express prejudice for a whole group of people based on a single anger-provoking event with one individual of particular ethnicity, race, or gender.

The many faces of anger below might be labeled as unhealthy, dysfunctional, clumsy, or immature. Whatever the label you assign them, you will probably agree that they are unproductive. The original cause of the anger in you or someone else might be worsened by these expressions of anger. Certainly, they add to bad feelings all around: more anger, frustration, and hopelessness.

Look at the faces of anger around you. Mark the list below with your name or someone else's.

Yelling	Brooding	Threats
Screaming	Bellowing	Insults
Swearing	Ranting	Demanding
Rapid talking	Raving	Manipulation
Contrariness	Tirades	Irritation
Sulking	Speeches	Tantrums

Martyrdom	Overeating	Name calling
Withdrawal	Self-mutilation	Insults
Stony silence	Spending money	Accusations
Resentment	Contempt	Ignoring people
Annoyance	Ridicule	Selective hearing
Procrastination	Eye rolling	Prejudice
Forgetting	Making faces	Gossip
Exhaustion	Sarcasm	Rumors
Sleepiness	Mean humor	Law suits
Headaches	Criticism	Revenge
Stomachaches	Fault-finding	Persuasion
Not eating	Tell someone off	Picking a fight
Body clenching	Lectures	Sabotage
Depression	Blaming	Blackmail
Self-medicating	Promiscuity	Guilt tripping
Drugs	Infidelity	
Alcohol	Sabotage	

Diagnosing (calling someone mentally ill, crazy, anal, obsessed)

_____

Withholding (money, love, affection, attention, sex)

_____

Accusing someone else of picking a fight

_____

Violence against property (smashing, breaking, or throwing things)

_____

Physical violence against people (hitting, smacking, pushing, beating, etc.)

_____

Physical violence against animals (kicking an animal)

_____

Add your own:

_____

Circle the words you use to express your own anger.

Fly off the handle	Flip out
Pitch a fit	Blow a gasket
Get bent out of shape	Lose your temper
Freak out	Have a short fuse
Lose it	Blow your cork
Bounce off the walls	Steamed
Have kittens	Go ape shit

34

Have a cow   Bent out of shape

Have a canary   Get unraveled

Boiling mad   Spitting nails

In a tailspin   Shitting bricks

Have a shit fit   Have a stroke

Go ballistic   In a lather

Jumping mad   Hit the ceiling

Mad as a hornet   Have a bee in your bonnet

Hot under the collar

(add your own) _____

_____

_____

Each of us has a choice of how to respond to our anger when it arises.

Each of us has a choice of how to respond to our anger when it arises. We can deny, repress, acknowledge, contain, express (appropriately), explode, take action based on our angry feelings, or some combination of these reactions, depending on the situation.

Deny. I'm not angry. I never get angry about anything. (Or I'm too spiritual to be angry.)

Repress. Uh-oh. I'm angry. I'd better not be angry. I'll push that feeling away. (Or I'll do something to get away from the feeling, such as having a drink or eating.)

Contain. I'm angry, but I will settle down and think this through. I don't want to say or do something I'll be sorry for later. I'll wait until this feeling passes before reacting.

Express (appropriately). I'm angry, and I have a right to say so. I can explain myself calmly and say what is bothering me without being hurtful or abusive.

Explode. I'm furious, and I'm not taking this for another second! I'm going to give them a piece of my mind! I'm going to throw something! (Some people explode into tears.)

Take action. This is unacceptable, and I'm going to do something to change things so I don't have to deal with this repeatedly. I'm going to call (or write to or tell) _____.

Acknowledge. I'm getting angry. I can feel it, and I accept that emotion. Now I can think about what I want to do with it.

IF ANGER WAS FORBIDDEN IN YOUR FAMILY

If anger was not permitted in your family, you can be sure that the repression has an effect on you today. People who have been constrained from expressing any anger at all soon become unable to recognize when they are angry and fear any expression of anger in others. In addition, they may suppress all their emotions so that they find themselves in a perpetually "numbed" state, moving through life like an automaton. These people are often seen as humorless or joyless; they may suffer from depression and chronic malaise.

If you can't express what you feel, then you may soon not even know what you feel. Language defines our experience. As adults, we may only know what we think and feel when we find words to say it. Writing helps us find our words.

> Language defines our experience. As adults, we may only know what we think and feel when we find words to say it. Writing helps us find our words.

If you think you don't get angry

If you believe you never get angry, I would suggest you re-read the section above and see if these possibilities apply to you. Remember that if you stuff down or repress all your anger, you are likely repressing your positive feelings as well. You can know you are angry without acting on it or showing it inappropriately. You can choose to separate your behavior from your thoughts or feelings.

IF ANGER WAS EXPRESSED TOO OPENLY IN YOUR FAMILY

In some households, anger is expressed strongly and frequently. It may come out as verbal abuse: name-calling, accusations, criticism, and put-downs. If you had a steady exposure to verbal abuse, you may have adopted this style of angry expression. On the other hand, you might be so repulsed by this kind of talk that you cannot stand any expression of anger at all.

Similarly, if you grew up in an atmosphere where physical abuse was common, whether directed against your personal property or against your person, your ability to deal with your anger or the anger of others will be affected. If you live with angry people now, you may be afraid that your anger will provoke them. Learning how to calmly express your own anger will help you to avoid triggering theirs.

Context determines whether or not your choice of expression is appropriate.

Context determines whether or not your choice of expression is appropriate.

!

1. Write down the first five (or more) things that make you angry. Don't ponder this; just write what pops into your mind. Circle the one thing that has the most angry charge for a closer look.

2. When you get angry, what do you tell yourself?

3. What do you do with the anger? Do you turn it inward or outward? How do you express it? How do you hold it in?

4. How do you feel about your anger? (Guilty? Ashamed? Proud?)

5. Are there times when you feel differently about your anger? What different kinds of anger do you experience? What situations provoke your anger?

6. Write about a specific event when you used each of the following strategies for dealing with anger.
   # Denial
   # Repression
   # Expression (appropriately)
   # Explosion
   # Action
   # Containment
   # Acknowledgment

   Which of these responses sounds like the way you handle anger most frequently?

7. What other emotions come up as you examine these different styles of anger?

8. If anger was forbidden in your family, how did this affect you?

9. How did you manage your anger as a child? As an adolescent? As a young adult? Now?

10. If anger was expressed too openly in your family with physical or verbal abuse, how has that affected your feelings about anger today?

11. Do you get angry at your own anger? Why?

Prompts

Choose the prompts that interest you most, and use the blank pages that follow to record your responses.

Revenge is a dish that tastes better cold.

Proverb

#

*

#

*

Meekness, n.
Uncommon patience
in planning a revenge
that is worthwhile.

Ambrose Bierce

Rage cannot be hidden;
it can only
be dissembled.

James Baldwin

chapter 4

JOURNALING ABOUT WHAT TICKS YOU OFF

If you have ever kept a journal for some period of time, you have probably noticed that much of what you write is negative and angry. It may sound whiny, petty, mean, gross, nasty, and trivial. But that's what a journal is for—it's a place where we don't have to be politically correct, polite, or articulate. We don't have to demonstrate good manners. The whole purpose of a journal is to let loose, to unload our feelings, worries, and frustrations, and to do it in a way that we wouldn't if we thought others were going to read it. Letting go of these negative thoughts and feelings in a journal gives us a safe place to speak our truths—even if they're only the temporary truths brought on by a bad mood or a headache.

We also have the opportunity to reflect on what we write. We can hear ourselves being chronically angry, depressed, or complaining, and we can choose to do something about those feelings we keep recycling in our journal. If you write for hours about your anger toward someone, you will likely see your own contribution to the situation. You might also decide to just let it go and stop wallowing in your feelings. Or you may conclude that you need to discuss it with the person or do something else to change the situation.

A CONTAINER FOR YOUR ANGER

Your journal provides a safe place for venting about what ticks you off. You don't have to worry about the consequences of what you write. Unless you make the mistake of sharing your journal with others, you can't hurt their feelings, provoke their anger at you, or give them cause to retaliate. Your journal provides a container for your anger, and while it isn't hermetically sealed, it can put you in touch with those parts of yourself that may not be suitable to broadcast publicly. It's a place where you can be true to yourself while making the conscious choice about how much needs to remain private. On paper and with a trusted friend, you might practice how to discuss what troubles you.

Benefits of ventilating anger

When you ventilate your anger by following the writing prompts, you will discover that you have a sense of greater mastery of your emotions: You can recognize them, accept them, and manage them in a way that is more acceptable to your own standards of expression. You will be able to understand yourself better. In particular, you will feel as if you understand the sources of your anger and the things that trigger its expression. Each of these levels of self-awareness will give you better self-control. If you feel you have been very self-controlled up until now and see that as a problem, gaining this greater understanding will allow you to consciously choose your style of self-control.

ANGER AS ENERGY TO BE REFOCUSED

You can imagine your anger as energy. For some people, anger certainly feels like a surge of energy. Maybe your face gets hot and you feel as if you have to move

Your journal provides a container for your anger, and while it isn't hermetically sealed, it can put you in touch with those parts of yourself that may not be suitable to broadcast publicly.

It is likely that whatever caused your anger in this moment has come your way before.

around or jump out of your seat. You may find that you gesture, shout, or are physical in some other way. Many people use physical exercise as a way to manage and subdue their anger. They clean and scrub their houses, jog, cycle, power walk, go to the gym, or work in the garden. They take their anger and refocus their attention and agitation onto something useful and productive. The energy associated with the anger is dissipated or exhausted in physical exertion.

Less healthy ways of releasing anger include getting into physical fights, destroying or vandalizing property, hurting yourself, or driving aggressively and recklessly.

If you are afraid of your anger and what you might do with it, you may perceive this surge of power and energy as negative. You might wonder if you're going crazy, or if you could be dangerous. You may perceive these feelings as something to get rid of.

Alternatively, you can see your anger as a gift or an opportunity. We've already seen how anger can be seen as a warning that something is wrong and needs changing. But you can also seize the energy surge and turn it into motivation—to do something that you have put off for too long. It is likely that whatever caused your anger in this moment has come your way before. When you get angry enough and energized enough, you can make a clear decision and carry it through. "Enough is enough!" turns into "I'm going to move, quit, find another job, stop wasting my time, get out of this unhealthy relationship, be choosier about picking my friends, take better care of myself, and register for school." You can take those old whines and put them into new casks.

!

1. Do you ever feel stuck in your anger? What do you do when you feel stuck?

2. In the past, what strategies have you used to release your anger?

3. Do you or does anyone you know wallow in anger? What are the signs of this?

4. What would you suggest to a friend who wallows in anger? How can you take your own advice?

5. When you feel angry, what is the first thing you want to do?

6. What are physical signals of your anger?

7. Has your anger ever propelled you toward a big decision? Describe.

8. Has your anger ever pushed you to do something you had put off? Describe.

9. Write down one thing in your life right now that ticks you off. What would have to happen to force you to do something about this?

10. How could you refocus or redirect the energy of your anger?

11. What would you like to do? What holds you back now?

12. How do you see your choices? (Healthy? Unhealthy? Cautious? Prudent? Chicken?)

13. How is your anger a gift?

Prompts

Choose the prompts that interest you most, and use the blank pages that follow to record your responses.

! @!*#@!!#**@#!#*!

Anger is a signal, and one worth listening to.

Harriet Lerner

*The best emotions to
write out of are anger
and fear and dread.*

Susan Sontag

part II
WHAT MAKES YOU ANGRY:
VENTILATE!

WHAT DRIVES YOU CRAZY

HOT BUTTONS AND TRIGGERS

We all have things that can set us off, and they can happen when we least expect them—driving, watching television, or overhearing a conversation.

Knowing your hot buttons and triggers—those things that set you off—whether you show your anger or not, can help you get a handle on these emotions. That awareness can also help you to understand and manage the emotions that create your anger.

Displaced anger: sweating the small stuff

Sometimes we get very angry over something trivial. We drop something, and then we swear and shout. We might fly into a rage because someone used our belongings or moved something from the place we expected to find it. We pitch a fit. We might say it is the last straw—enough is enough! If we give it any thought, we know that we are really angry about something else. This event (or non-event) just put us over the edge. Maybe we've been angry about something else that we aren't fully aware of or are afraid to talk about. Maybe our anger has nothing to do with the present situation. We have displaced the anger onto this situation when it really should be directed elsewhere.

53

We can calm ourselves by thinking about the problem differently, and we can choose not to say hurtful things or retaliate in other ways when we are hurt and angry.

Delayed anger: furious a day late

We might also delay our anger. Maybe we are angry with someone for something they did last week or last year. Then, when we are together, we get furious over something trivial. When we finally reveal our anger, it may have been brewing for some time. Maybe we were collecting our evidence or cataloging our grievances. Instead of showing an emotional reaction that fits the current circumstances, we pop off because we are angry about something from the past. The anger is delayed rather than displaced.

Within my control

Although feelings seem to sweep over us uncontrollably, we have more control than we think. We can calm ourselves by viewing the problem from a different angle, and we can choose not to say hurtful things or retaliate in other ways when we are hurt and angry. We can choose to walk away or remove ourselves emotionally from the events that trigger our anger. In many ways, we create our feelings. We'll look at this concept more in Part III.

Not in my control

However, many of us get angry, or at least irritated, about things that are not in our control. We plan a picnic in the park, and it rains. We decide to spend our day off at the beach, and we spend it packing to evacuate for a hurricane instead. We invest money in a company, and the supplier goes out of business or the stock crashes. Batteries run out, water pipes break, tornadoes touch ground, and traffic lights turn red. Perhaps most frustrating of all—and not the least bit in our control—are other people, especially those who are close to us and those we love. People drive drunk, take drugs, squander their paychecks, and allow themselves to be mistreated. The most we can do is calmly offer support and concern—especially to our children. But they won't even be able to hear us if we are angry.

Choose the prompts that interest you most, and use the blank pages that follow to record your responses.

1. Make a quick list of twenty-five things that tick you off.

2. Look at your list. Do the items fall into three or four categories? What are they? What do these categories tell you?

3. For the next week, notice when you are teed off and add to this list. Nothing is too absurd, inappropriate, silly, or irrational. If you get angry, just write it down. Your feelings are your feelings, no matter what they are.

4. Write about a time when your anger was delayed.

5. Write about a time when your anger was displaced.
   # What did you tell yourself about the circumstances of the original event that made you hold back from speaking your truth?
   # When you finally showed your anger, what was the trigger? What would you do differently now?

6. What makes you angry but is also in your power to control or change?

7. What choices have you made in the past that have caused your anger today?

8. Of the things that make you angry, list those that are not at all in your control. (Consider these carefully since you often have more influence and control than you recognize.)

9. What makes people you know angry when it's clear to you that they can't do anything about it?

10. What do others do with their lives that makes you angry, but you know what you say has no effect?

11. What makes you angry about yourself that you can't change? (Your height? Metabolism? Race? Intelligence? Age? Physical limitations?)

*I love being married. It's
so great to find that one
special person you want
to annoy for the rest of
your life.*

Rita Rudner

\#

!

@

!

*

\#

?

Anger as soon as fed is dead
'Tis starving makes it fat.

Emily Dickinson

chapter 6

HOT BUTTONS AT WORK

Getting ticked off at work seems like part of having a job—any job. Co-workers drive you crazy with their incompetence and stupidity; many of the tasks you have to do are unpleasant or boring, and sometimes a job can feel like you're doing time. Or maybe you really are on your way to hell and this is a sample of what it will be like.

Anger on the job can be particularly distressing—it's hard to be candid and truthful about what's bothering you if you think you might be fired. Even if you don't feel your job is at risk when you want to express your anger appropriately, you may be concerned that someone might use it against you later.

Ventilating in your journal won't have any of those consequences, so let it rip.

!

1. What aspects of your work do you hate to do? List.

2. Are there others who like the tasks you hate? Who are they?

3. List the people at work who tick you off. (You can use real names. This is your personal journal. Just don't carry it to work with you!) What do they do that ticks you off? What category do most of them fall in? (Supervisors? Co-workers? Rivals? Employees?)

4. What rules and red tape tick you off?

5. Do you get the recognition you deserve at work? If not, write about what you would like to see changed.

6. In detail, give three examples that capture your anger at work. What do you notice? Any pattern?

7. Does writing about these events make you feel better or worse? (If you feel worse immediately after writing, notice how you feel after a few days.) If you feel more angry after writing than before, what does it tell you about how to manage your anger?

8. Choose one of the examples you wrote about anger at work and write it again from someone else's point of view. (Choose someone who is likely to see it differently.) How did they perceive the situation? What does their anger tell you they need?

9. What conditions on your job tick you off?

10. If you had the power, what would you change in your company to make it run better?
    # What would you change about the organization of your company?
    # What would you change about the way your company treats people?

Choose the prompts that interest you most, and use the blank pages that follow to record your responses.

Prompts

What can you do to increase your power and influence at work?

11. How are you a "secret star" in your workplace?

12. How would you like to be more appreciated? What can you do to make this happen?

You will not be
punished for your anger;
you will be punished by
your anger.

Buddha

@ * # * $ * ! * @ *

* # * $ * ! * @

\# *

Anger makes dull men witty,
but it keeps them poor.

Sir Francis Bacon

chapter 7

HOT BUTTONS AT HOME AND IN YOUR PERSONAL LIFE

As at work, so at home. A man's home is his castle, but too often, it feels like his hovel. Running your own life means managing a household, a car, and a hundred appliances that your great-grandparents couldn't have imagined. Modern technology means we are more mobile and can communicate (by e-mail, telephones, fax machines, beepers, cell phones) with more people every day, vastly amplifying the mental demands that our brains and emotions were designed to endure. No wonder we're ticked off!

PEOPLE WHO DRIVE YOU CRAZY: OH, THE THINGS THEY DO!

If your co-workers don't drive you crazy, then those in your family and those you live with will surely jump in to do their duty. Sometimes it seems that the people who know you the longest have the best tactics for ticking you off. If you have children, you can probably write a whole book on what kids can do to make you angry.

*Write names of people who tick you off in the space below
each of the following categories.*

Spouse/mate/lover(s)
_____

Ex-spouse(s)
_____

Ex-lover(s)
_____

Parents (or those who raised you)
_____

Grandparents
_____

Siblings (brother, sister, half- and step-siblings)
_____

Family (cousins, aunts, uncles)
_____

Children
_____

Friends
_____

Neighbors
_____

Classmates (current)
_____

Classmates (former)
_____

Professionals (doctor, lawyer, dentist, therapist)
_____

Landlord (or tenants)
_____

Adversaries
_____

Competitors

_____

Enemies

_____

Users, takers, and exploiters

_____

Cheapskates

_____

Liars

_____

Cheaters

_____

ANGER WORKSHEET

Person's name:

_____

What does this person do to tick me off?

This person

_____

This person

_____

This person

_____

What does this person say to tick me off?

This person says

_____

This person says

_____

This person says

_____

What does this tell me about what this other person needs?

This person needs _____

This person needs _____

This person needs _____

What do *I* want this person to do?

I wish this person would _____

I wish this person would _____

I wish this person would _____

What does this worksheet tell me *I* need?

I need _____

I need _____

I need _____

!

74

Choose the prompts that interest you most, and use the blank pages that follow to record your responses.

1. What drives you crazy in your home environment?

2. What chores do you hate to do? (Make the list as long as you like. No one is going to argue with you.)

3. Look over your list of chores and tasks. What can you delegate to other family members?

4. If you had trouble with the idea of delegation, what holds you back? Explain what you believe would happen.

5. What can you do to simplify your tasks? (Cook in bulk? Clean piecemeal?)

6. Can you lower your standards to make it easier on yourself? (Change your bed sheets or wash the car less often?)

7. Can you afford to hire help to do some tasks? (Taking out prepared food? Having a person clean your house—or only one part of it—once a month?) Explain how you might budget for this.

8. List the technological "advances" in your life that tyrannize you (e.g., telephone, beeper, etc.). Which of these can you do without?
   # How will you feel without them? (Unburdened? Liberated? Disconnected? Fearful?)
   # How might you change the way you use these technological wonders so they are more helpful than burdensome in your life?

9. Make a list of all the things you did in the last twenty-four hours. How much did you get accomplished? Include even the smallest tasks, such as unloading the dishwasher or returning phone calls.

10. Make a list of all those people who tick you off.
    # For each person, fill out the worksheet on pages 72-73. What do you learn from this process?
    # Pick a name from your list, and write one short story about an interaction that ticked you off or frustrated you.
    # Look over your story, and ask yourself what you wanted to be different. Write that down as a clear request.
    # If you were a comedian, how might you retell these stories adding humor and insight?

76 | *The more you love, the more you can love—and the more intensely you love. Nor is there any limit on how many you can love. If a person had time enough, he could love all of that majority who are decent and just.*

Robert A. Heinlein

Don't hold on to anger, hurt or pain. They steal your energy and keep you from love.

Leo Buscaglia

chapter 8

WORLD AFFAIRS: WHAT'S IN THE NEWS

It's been said that news isn't news unless it's bad news. It must dramatize, frighten, or provoke worry. In many ways, the news and talk shows are meant to tick you off, because a change in your emotional balance grabs your attention.

!

1. For each of the issues below, write your thoughts and emotional reactions in just a few words.

Abortion

Sex education

Gun control

Crime

Racism

Healthcare

Child care

Elder care

Child abuse

Education

School prayer

Science vs. religion

Immigration

Gay issues (in the military, gay marriage, scouting)

Drug use

Legalization of drugs

Environmental issues

Animal rights

Domestic abuse

Prompts

Choose the prompts that interest you most, and use the blank pages that follow to record your responses.

Prompts

Violence and sex in movies and television

Monogamy vs. non-monogamy

Taxes

Prison reform

Euthanasia

Private property rights

Inflation

Interest rates

Mergers and big business

Censorship

Flag burning

Other

As you responded to these, which ones made you want to write a lot more? Circle them and make some notes while you're having strong reactions. You can come back to them later.

2. What news stories tick you off?

3. Do you ever find yourself shouting at the television set? (This is OK as long as the television doesn't talk back.) What do you say?

4. What exactly creates your anger? (The way the story is told? The content? Your disagreement?) Specify with an example.

5. If you were in political power, what is the first thing you would do?

6. What news stories do you find the most distressing?

7. When have you turned off the television or radio when hearing a news story?

8. How can you translate your anger into something useful and productive? (Write letters to the newspaper or your congressperson; organize others to write, march, or file a class action suit; educate others about the issue; volunteer to teach reading or to help at a soup kitchen.)

9. Behind our anger, there are often other feelings, especially fear, sadness, and despair. For the issues below that tick you off, what is the heartbreak behind your anger?
   # Wars
   # Refugees
   # Famines
   # Natural disasters
   # Manmade disasters (oil spills, pollution, deforestation, extinction of species)
   # Other heartbreaking stories—what issues affect you?

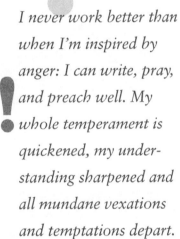

I never work better than when I'm inspired by anger: I can write, pray, and preach well. My whole temperament is quickened, my under-standing sharpened and all mundane vexations and temptations depart.

Martin Luther

• • • • • • • • •

Man invented language
to satisfy his deep need
to complain.

Lily Tomlin

chapter 9

LET US BLESS IRREVERENCE

One man's theology is another man's belly laugh.

Robert Heinlein

Each of us holds certain values dear. We may believe that only certain kinds of behavior and thoughts are moral, acceptable, ethical, or proper. We know our beliefs are the right ones. And everyone else believes the same thing— except that their beliefs are often very different from ours, or even the direct opposite! How can they think that? And what's worse, they want us to change our beliefs to their beliefs. We wouldn't dream of doing that! Or would we?

!

Choose the prompts that interest you most, and use the blank pages that follow to record your responses.

1. Who has tried to evangelize to you or convert you?
   # What did the person do? How did you react?
   # How do you wish you had reacted?
   # What do you think you'll do next time?

2. Have religious groups called your home or sent you literature to convert you? What did you do in each case?

3. Do you have a friend or family member who is trying to convert you to their religious (or non-religious) beliefs? Name him or her (or them). What did this person do?
   # What does this person want you to do or understand?
   # What is his/her intent?

4. Indulge in an inappropriate fantasy: what would you like to have said and done to a person who tried to evangelize to you? (Write it out, and let it rip. It's just a fantasy. You can imagine yourself answering the door naked.)
   # How do you feel after writing this fantasy? If you're not laughing, what happened?

5. What is the basis for your personal morality and ethical principles? Write it in a few sentences.

Believe nothing, no matter where you read it, or who said it, no matter if I have said it, unless it agrees with your own reason and your own common sense.

Buddha

A competent and self-confident person is incapable of jealousy in anything. Jealousy is invariably a symptom of neurotic insecurity.

Robert A. Heinlein

chapter 10

WHEN YOU FEEL LIKE A VICTIM

Into every life a little rain must fall.

OK. So sometimes you get a monsoon. And maybe that's followed by a tidal wave. You get more than you think you deserve. You're off the scales of all stress tests, and your car just died on the interstate. It seems as if everything is going wrong.

It isn't fair, and it makes you hoppin' mad!

BAD DRIVERS

In my conversations with people about what ticks them off, bad drivers are the most frequent response. People who run red lights and stop signs, weave in and out of traffic, speed, cut you off, and drive drunk also drive us crazy. What are they doing?

CRIMINALS AND THE JUSTICE SYSTEM

More cops, more jails, more courts, more lawyers, and more jails. Where does it end? If you've ever had a face-off with the criminal justice system, you may have felt like a victim no matter what side of the law you were on. How many innocent people go to jail? How many criminals don't?

PRODUCT BETRAYALS

And now, let us buy. Later we will pay.

The shoddy quality of the goods we purchase ticks a lot of people off. Either your new product is replaced by a newer model before you get it home, or it breaks long before you thought it should. If you purchase merchandise, shouldn't it last? Doesn't it tick you off to know that manufactured goods—in this country, as well as others—are made to break?

PERSONAL BETRAYALS

Being betrayed by someone you trust can really make you feel like a victim. If you've ever invested time, energy, and love in a relationship and been dumped, you know how much that hurts. Or when the person we thought was a monogamous partner cheats on us, we may feel especially betrayed. Broken agreements and broken contracts of any kind can feel like betrayals.

JEALOUSY

Jealousy is one kind of anger. It says, "You're mine. I'm not sharing you. How dare you be affectionate with someone else!"

Being human includes being jealous occasionally, especially when we feel threatened at the prospect of losing the love or attention of someone we are committed to. Some evolutionary psychologists say that jealousy is one way to keep our genes in the gene pool and to insure—for the man—that the children he raises are his own. Using our conscious minds and the technology of birth control, we can say that we will be careful not to bring unwanted children into the world, but we may still get jealous to see our lover flirting with someone else.

These feelings, whether you think they are reasonable or not, can spark anger.

BROKEN PROMISES AND VIOLATIONS OF TRUST

Broken promises can lead to jealousy, but outside of a romantic context, they might lead to other feelings of anger such as outrage, shock, disappointment, distrust, and fear. If you've been promised something—or thought you were—then you might feel very ticked off when that promise is broken. If you trusted someone with your money, your secrets, your vulnerability, or your property, you may feel angry if this person violates your trust.

GETTING SUED

If you've ever been sued or been threatened with a lawsuit, you know how much that can tick you off. Perhaps you did someone a favor by offering your professional advice free of charge, and now he wants to sue you for malpractice. Or you had a party at your home, and someone drank too much and slipped on your walkway on the way out. Then she tries to hold you responsible—in court. Even if you win the suit, it will cost you money and energy to defend yourself. That's sure to tick you off.

!

Choose the prompts that interest you most, and use the blank pages that follow to record your responses.

1. What ticks you off when you're driving? What do you usually do?

2. Are you prone to road rage? What can you do to defuse this pattern of reactivity?

3. Have you ever felt like a victim in the criminal justice system?

4. Have you ever been arrested? What crimes have you gotten away with?

5. Have you ever been the victim of a crime? (Burglary? Mugging? Theft? Something even more violent?) What did you learn from that experience?

6. What products have betrayed you? If you could have a private talk with Ralph Nader, what would you like to see him focus on next?

7. Who has broken an agreement or a promise to you? What happened?

8. What is betrayal?

9. Who has betrayed you? What happened? (Write the story.)
   # How has this affected your other relationships?
   # What have you done to resolve this sense of betrayal?
   # Is there another way to tell this story?

10. Whom have you betrayed?

11. Write about a time when you were intensely jealous. What did you do with your jealousy?

12. How is jealousy a sign of your insecurity? What would be your ideal reaction to your own feelings of jealousy?

Prompts

13. Write about your partner's jealousy—past or present.

14. Who has broken a promise to you? How did you feel? What did you do?

15. Who has violated your trust? How did you feel? What did you do?

16. If you have ever had someone bring a lawsuit against you, did it tick you off? If yes, why?

17. What other events have led to you feeling like a victim?

It takes your enemy and your friend, working together, to hurt you to the heart; the one to slander you and the other to get the news to you.

Mark Twain

Living well is the best revenge.

Proverb

As a girl my temper often got out of bounds. But one day when I became angry at a friend over some trivial matter, my mother said to me, "Elizabeth, anyone who angers you conquers you."

Elizabeth Kenny

part III

TRANSFORMING AND USING ANGER PRODUCTIVELY

chapter 11

MANAGING YOUR ANGER

What makes you angry? You do.

Yes. You do.

You make yourself angry. Yes, this sounds like a contradiction to all the phrasing in Parts I and II of this book. Throughout, I've used the common wording that something "ticks you off"—as if the events occurring outside you create your feelings. But external events don't create your feelings—you do.

THOUGHTS CREATE FEELINGS

Between the event and the resulting anger, we may have irrational thoughts such as:

Reasonable people shouldn't do that.
People should be more careful!
You should know that would hurt my feelings.
I expected to be treated a certain way and I wasn't.
My talents and skills should be acknowledged.
If I have to ask you do this for me, then it doesn't count.

For many people, anger is a screen emotion. Behind the screen are other emotions that are harder to accept.

Notice all the *shoulds* in the previous statements. We assume that others have the same expectations we have and that they will honor them. When our expectations are not met, we get angry.

Your power to attribute meaning to the events of your life can make you happy or miserable. It's your choice. You can read malice into other people's actions and get very ticked off, or you can assume that the other person wasn't intentionally trying to hurt you. (Of course, you could get ticked off at the possibility that the other person wasn't thinking about you, but that's only because you think he *should* have been thinking about you—a belief that creates your anger.) Like you, he was likely thinking about himself!

Therefore, our thoughts and beliefs make us angry. We do it to ourselves. It's not what other people do that makes us angry; it's how we interpret what they do. By attributing malice, ignorance, or willful neglect to other people's actions, we make ourselves angry. By demanding others be different from who they are, we fuel our angry feelings.

We hold the power to choose some other explanation. We can put another spin on the events, reframe them, or explain them in a way that might even be flattering to ourselves—which might be equally untrue, but might, at least, sting less. (For example, your boss didn't promote you because he's afraid you'll shine and take over his job.)

For many people, anger is a screen emotion. Behind the screen are other emotions that are harder to accept. Give an example when you reacted in anger to "screen" the following emotions. For example, you may be angry with a teenage child for staying out late, but your real feelings are worry and fear for his safety.

SCREEN EMOTION	REAL EMOTION
Fear	_____
Terror	_____
Hurt	_____
Grief	_____
Disappointment	_____
Anxiety	_____
Desire	_____
Lust	_____
Jealousy	_____

MOVING BEYOND ANGER

Getting past your anger means that you approach a situation with a different point of view. Sometimes, you may have to ventilate in your journal before you can move beyond your anger. Psychologically, you can say you need "closure." The pathway to closure may be any of the strategies below, and they may follow in different orders for different people.

Accept

For us to come to terms with our anger so that we don't fly off and break things or hurt people, we must first accept that we are angry. Accepting your anger doesn't mean that you have to do anything about it. It may not even make sense to you that you feel angry. You just know you feel it. No judgment or action is necessary.

Avoid

Knowing what makes us angry—or rather, that at certain times we are more likely to make ourselves angry—we can choose to avoid the provocation. We can make the conscious decision to avoid those people, events, circumstances, or information that raise our anger. We can say to ourselves, "I don't want to have dinner with so-and-so. She is negative most of the time, and that makes me angry."

Detach

One of the reasons why we get ticked off is that we are attached to an outcome. We want things a certain way. We want people to behave in a certain way. If we detach from our insistence that there is only one acceptable outcome, we are less likely to be angry when we don't get what we want. We can say, "It doesn't matter. Whatever happens, I'll deal with it."

Dispute

When we examine our beliefs and expectations that fueled our anger to begin with, we can choose to think differently. Perhaps, as a child, I expected my parents to know everything and always act in my best interest. This belief or expectation is irrational. My parents were humans too, flawed and limited as we all are. Knowing the irrational beliefs that fuel my anger, I can dispute their accuracy.

Forgive

We can also move beyond anger through forgive-

Trying to forgive first may not work for you. And there are those who say that some things are unforgivable.

ness. Knowing that no one is perfect, that others make mistakes, that like us, they are sometimes dense or ignorant, we can forgive their blunders—including those mistakes that hurt us.

However, it is possible to fall into what Susan Forward, author of *Toxic Parents*, has called "the forgiveness trap." If you try to deny your anger and stuff it down because you feel guilty about your anger and want to be "properly forgiving," then you may not even allow yourself anger that is justified. People who think of themselves as spiritually evolved usually want to forgive instead of allowing themselves to be angry.

Your anger doesn't mean you have to get revenge or confront the other person. It means you can accept your anger and then forgive the person who hurt you. Trying to forgive first may not work for you. And there are those who say that some things are unforgivable. Only you can decide what falls in that category.

Remember to forgive yourself, too: for making mistakes out of ignorance and immaturity, for being persuaded by foolish people, and for allowing yourself to be mistreated by others. You did the best you could do at the time.

Write unsent letters

Another way to move beyond anger is to write letters and not send them. In your journal, you can write a long letter to the person—living or dead—who has angered you. In this letter, you get to say all the things you would like to say, no matter how offensive and hurtful your words are, knowing he or she will never read it. Hold nothing back; say it all. The letter stays in your journal where it remains between you and yourself. Alternatively, you can burn the letter or read it aloud to the universe in a ritual for closure, but don't send the letter to the target of your anger. You might want to use Susan Forward's guidelines for writing a confrontational letter (which is sometimes the appropriate choice). The four elements are:

1. This is what you did to me.
2. This is how I felt at the time.
3. This is how it affected my life.
4. This is what I want from you now.

Resist the urge to mail this letter—even if you have an address to mail it to. If, after you cool down and can think more clearly, you decide you still want to write a letter to the person, start again and write a letter that you can send, and that will benefit both of you. Keep your wide-ranging ventilating to yourself.

If you are writing to someone deceased, don't try writing your letter on asbestos with the intention of sending it where you think your target now resides. Mail service hasn't gone all to hell yet.

Prompts

1. Look back over the writing you've done in the first two-thirds of this book. What emotions might have been behind the anger? List and explain.

2. What does "moving beyond anger" mean to you? Write about an event that demonstrates your acceptance of your own anger in a specific situation.

3. What situations would you be better off avoiding because you are so often angry in them?

4. How can you escape situations that raise your anger?

5. What irrational beliefs lead to your anger? (Look for sentences with *should, always,* and *never* in them.) Give an example of disputing your irrational beliefs.

6. Whom do you need to forgive as a way of getting complete with your anger?

7. In what ways do you need to forgive yourself?

8. Make a list of people who are good candidates for unsent letters. Then, write the opening sentences for three of these letters. (You're not going to mail them!)

   Dear _____

   _____

   Dear _____

   _____

   Dear _____

   _____

9. In what way is your anger unproductive? How does it make things worse for you?

10. How is your anger making you sick?

11. What else can you do to get complete with your anger?

Beware the fury of a
patient man.

John Dryden

It is hard to fight an enemy who has outposts in your head.

Sally Kempton

{ ! ! ! ! ! ! ! ! ! }

Anger is a symptom, a way of cloaking and expressing feelings too awful to experience directly—hurt, bitterness, grief and, most of all, fear.

Joan Rivers

chapter 12

USING WHAT YOU LEARN ABOUT YOURSELF

Examining our anger patterns helps us see how much of what we say and do is automatic. We may not have realized the thoughts behind our anger. We may not have considered that the stories we made up about the intentions and motivations of others are only that: stories we made up.

By learning about your anger patterns and how you tick yourself off, you can take greater responsibility for your emotions and what you do with them.

If we want to make peace and foster serenity in ourselves and others, we can take responsibility for being more peaceful (instead of fueling our own anger and that of others with accusations and blame).

FEELING HELPLESS OR DEPRESSED

Sometimes anger can lead to feeling helpless or depressed. This seems to be especially common for women, who are trained to swallow their anger (to literally or figuratively eat it). But even those feelings of powerlessness can be a signal to ask yourself whether you're angry instead of depressed and sad. If you are afraid your anger might get out of control, you may stifle any feelings of anger, and then be "blue" instead. Asking yourself what you can do may help.

For men, this situation may be reversed. Men may be willing to feel and show anger, but not depression or helplessness.

BOUNDARIES AND ASSERTIVENESS

Many of us get angry when we feel that we have been abused, exploited, used, or manipulated in some way.

People who violate your boundaries often don't have any of their own. They intrude into your physical and psychological space because they haven't learned to value their own. By setting boundaries and limits with others, you will feel as if you have more power and are less likely to get angry or depressed. You can openly state what you will not tolerate ("You can't smoke pot or cigarettes while you're a guest in my house"), how you expect to be treated ("I will expect you to call if you're going to be late"), or what your limits are ("I'm willing to help with the mailing, but I don't want to take full responsibility for this project"). By asserting yourself, you can feel more in control of your time and choices. When you say no to others, you say yes to yourself and what is important to you.

You can also set limits by what you do. By turning off your phone when you take a nap or by not taking your phone with you when you take a quiet walk, you are asserting your need for solitude and silence. You are telling others that you value yourself.

Your assertive actions and statements will serve as a good example of boundary setting for your children and family as well. When you set limits and say no, you give others permission to say no, too—to scoundrels, crooks, and others who wish them harm.

OTHERS AS MIRRORS

Sometimes, the people who irk us the most are those people who mirror our worst traits—the ones we don't want to own. When they are arrogant, selfish, indifferent, and cruel, we are reminded of how we behave in these ways.

Asking yourself how this particularly anger-provoking person is a mirror can provide an opportunity for insight and growth, as well as defusing your anger.

TRANSFORMING ENVY AND JEALOUSY

Envy might be behind your anger, too. Do you get angry at people whom you envy? Perhaps you want what they have or the success they have achieved. If you feel jealous of others, that could tell you that you are afraid of what you might lose.

After you identify what you yearn for, you might see the targets of your anger differently. Their success might now be the start of seeing them as role models and calls to excellence. Alternatively, you may see them as anti-role models if you don't want to achieve success in the same way they arrived at it.

ANGER DIARY

Redford and Virginia Williams (authors of *Anger Kills*), and other authors suggest keeping an anger diary as a way of becoming more aware of your anger style. This is one way to see your own patterns and decide how you want to make changes to reduce your hostility, cynicism, and aggression. Think about the questions below in your anger diary:

Trigger (What made you angry?)
Brief description of event (Who? What? Where?)

> By setting boundaries and limits with others, you will feel as if you have more power and are less likely to get angry or depressed.

The intensity of your anger (On a scale of 1–10?)
Duration of anger (One minute? One century?)
Frequency (How many times per week/month does this trigger set you off?)
Your thoughts (I think I over-reacted; I think I was justified.)
Your other feelings (What was under the anger? Fear? Hurt?)
Your actions (How did you express your anger?)
Outcome (Did you feel better or worse after your response? Was problem resolved? How?)
Hindsight—use what you learned (Next time I can-wait until I cool down before reacting.)

Prompts

Choose the prompts that interest you most, and use the blank pages that follow to record your responses.

1. When do you feel helpless?

2. When do you feel depressed?

3. Do these situations make you angry? How?

4. What can you do to make a change in this pattern?

5. How do you eat your anger?

6. Who violates your boundaries?

7. What can you do to assert your boundaries and limits? List at least three actions

8. What can you say to assert your boundaries and limits? Write three clear statements here like the ones suggested in the text.

9. Throughout this book, you've named several people who tick you off. Choose three who tick you off the most. Look at the worst traits you listed for them. Write how each of them is a mirror for your own defects, deficiencies, and weaknesses. (Yes, this is hard! Do it anyway.)

10. Of whom are you jealous or envious?

11. What does your envy and jealousy teach you about yourself? How can you use this to excel in ways you have not?

12. In a short paragraph (or more), write what taking personal responsibility means to you.

13. How can you put these words into action? Name two things you can do.

14. Using the guidelines for keeping an anger diary, adapt it to your specific needs, and keep your own for the next week or more.

Great artists treasure their time with a bitter and snarling miserliness.

Catherine D. Bowen

*If you are patient in one
moment of anger, you
will escape a hundred
days of sorrow.*

Chinese Proverb

In the midst of great joy, do not promise anyone anything. In the midst of great anger, do not answer anyone's letter.

Chinese Proverb

chapter 13

INFLUENCING OTHERS

I like long walks, especially when
they are taken by people
who annoy me.

Noel Coward

When we understand our actions, our thought patterns, and the origins of our emotions, we can make choices about what to do. By reducing our impulsive reactions, we can interact with others in ways that change how they respond to us. By communicating honestly and clearly with respect and consideration, we can influence others to treat us with more respect and consideration.

THOSE WHO DRIVE ME NUTS

When you review the people who drive you nuts, you may see a pattern emerge. Perhaps there are more people of one gender, or they are mostly at work, or mostly of a particular personality type. By knowing your own patterns, you can choose to relate to others differently.

If one of the things that ticks you off is that no one listens to you or takes you seriously, you might ask yourself how your talk makes others shut their ears. Perhaps your volume, tone, or vocabulary makes people shrink. People who are taken seriously and respected are those who respect themselves.

THE ART OF LISTENING

We all complain about how others don't listen, but how well do we listen to others? Real listening means that we stop composing in our heads. We really try to hear, see, and feel what the other person is describing. We ask questions to understand and get more information. We don't interpret or scold. We make a sincere effort to enter the other's experience, even if we disagree with the person's methods or beliefs. You might say:

I'm not getting the whole picture yet. Tell me more.
How did you interpret that?
How did that affect you?
I missed a part. Go back and explain that again for me.
I'm a little unclear about _____.

Listening includes being present at an emotional level. That means feeling empathy and compassion for the other person's experience. We can let others know that we have empathy by describing our own emotions as we listen: "That would have terrified me" or "I would have been so worried and sad" or "That must have been so exciting and wonderful!" We can show our compassion by relating those emotions back to the speaker: "You must be so relieved" or "You've been in my thoughts a lot lately."

SUGGESTING CHANGE

If a person's behavior is the frequent cause of our anger, we can ask them to make a change. While asking someone to change is usually an unreasonable or irrational demand, we can sometimes request a specific change of something that is a frequent focus of our anger (Could you please call if you're going to be late?). Keeping the request small and clear will make it more likely to be honored.

Prompts

Choose the prompts that interest you most, and use the blank pages that follow to record your responses.

1. What was your first thought when you saw this chapter's title?

2. List the people who drive you nuts or who you wish would listen to you.

3. Examine your style of delivery. What do you do that makes it hard for others to listen to you?

4. How might you better listen to others? Write down a few reminders of how you can do this (e.g., I'll be quiet when they speak and ask for clarification instead of jumping in).

5. Describe one incident when you showed empathy to another person.

6. What does compassion mean to you?

7. List five people who are role models for compassion and empathy.

8. Write down five statements you could make to another that would demonstrate your empathy.

9. Describe one incident when changing your own behavior changed how another treated you.

10. What small change can you make in your communication style that might change how others respond to you (e.g., a change in tone, pitch, vocabulary, volume, or gesture)?

11. Make a list of small behavior changes that you can ask for in others. (Also be open to their requests of you!)

● ● ●

*No person is important
enough to make me
angry.*

Carlos Castaneda

When I started, I wrote about hate and bitterness. Eventually, I threw those songs away, but the experience was better than a psychiatrist and a whole lot cheaper.

Jane Howard

chapter 14

CONVERTING ANGER INTO USEFUL ACTION

We have seen how feeling ticked off can be a gift—a signal that we need to make a change. You can take the insights you have about your anger and put them into action.

CHANGING YOURSELF

Starting change by changing yourself is a good place to begin. You can do that by changing what you think and what you do. Changing the stories you tell yourself and the attributions you give to any set of events will change your feelings. By changing your actions, you will feel different about yourself.

CONVERTING ANGER TO MOTIVATION

You can take the energy surge of anger and turn it into useful action. If you are really angry, you can do something. The greater your anger, the more energy you have to make changes and influence others. Your displeasure and outrage can be a source of motivation to take action, both individually and politically.

Activism and political change

One way to take action is through activism. When people are angry enough, they write to their representatives or march on Washington, D.C.; they form associations and clubs to educate others; they write plays, books, and television scripts to get their message out.

When Candy Lightner's twelve-year-old daughter Cari was killed by a drunk driver, she could have withdrawn into her grief and spent the rest of her life in bitterness and mourning. Instead, she started Mothers Against Drunk Drivers (MADD), a powerful group that has not only changed the laws and penalties for drunk driving across the nation, but has also been influential in changing the way we think about alcohol use.

Similarly, after John Walsh lost his son Adam, and Marc Klaas lost his daughter Polly, they mobilized more effective systems to track missing children and sought to educate people about the possible ways to prevent kidnapping.

By using the power surges behind their anger, these people turned their tragedies into triumphs—and made a real difference in the world. You can too.

The desire to make a difference doesn't have to stem from tragedy. If watching the evening news raises your anger, ask yourself what you can do—lobby, write letters, volunteer, and inform others. If you're shy about writing letters or doubt your ability to be articulate, write your first draft here or in a separate journal where you know you don't have to share it. You might change your mind and send it after you see what you have to say.

If you're shy about writing letters or doubt your ability to be articulate, write your first draft here or in a separate journal where you know you don't have to share it.

!

Prompts

Choose the prompts that interest you most, and use the blank pages that follow to record your responses.

1. What have you changed about yourself in doing the exercises in this book?

2. What other ways have you changed?

3. How is your anger a gift?

4. How can you convert your anger into motivation to do something?

5. What does you anger tell you to change?

6. What can you do with your anger that would make it useful?

7. How would you like the world to change?

8. What's the smallest thing you can do to begin to make that happen?

9. Of the things that make you angriest, how can you turn them into activism or political action?

10. Did you ever want to write a letter to your newspaper? Write a few paragraphs now, even if it's an old issue. (A few sentences will get you rolling and can begin your own political movement.)

11. What political groups or movements touch your heart? List three.

12. What can you do to participate in their efforts? (Contribute time? Money? Skill?)

If you can't annoy
somebody, there's little
point in writing.

Kingsley Amis

!

*Every action must be
due to one or other of
seven causes: chance,
nature, compulsion,
habit, reasoning, anger,
or appetite.*

Aristotle

*I have learned, through
bitter experience, the
one supreme lesson to
conserve my anger, and
as heat conserved is
transmitted into energy,
even so our anger
controlled can be trans-
mitted into a power that
can move the world.*

Mahatma Gandhi

chapter 15

FROM HERE TO SERENITY

Perhaps serenity is just another word for the happiness we all hope to achieve. You can do things in your daily life to raise your level of serenity by making your days more peaceful, quiet, and loving. You can choose to make changes, even if they seem difficult at first.

NURTURING OURSELVES

There are many ways you can nurture yourself to deal with what ticks you off. Beyond ventilating and writing about the sources of your anger, you can cultivate your own serenity. See my Web site at www.joanmazza.com for 101 ways to nurture yourself.

Ritual. To let go of an old anger, plan a simple ritual. You can bury or burn a symbol of your anger and read your letter to the winds, thereby returning the object and what it represents to the earth's elements. Rituals can transform your anger into other emotions: peace, forgiveness, sadness. Rituals help us to move into the next stage.

Stress busters. Use the techniques that work for you to reduce stress. Common practices include yoga, meditation, prayer, rest, listening to classical music, and petting your dog or cat.

Centering. Close your eyes and be with your feelings. Feel yourself as solid, sensible, and sane.

Breathe. Close your eyes and breathe.

Baths. Take a warm bath and let all your frustrations and irritations wash away. Watch them go down the drain. (You might want to try a bath in darkness or by candlelight if you find this more soothing.)

Exercise. Begin a regular program of exercise to release stress and tension in your body. If you haven't been exercising, you can start with a daily walk for fifteen minutes.

Simplify. Find ways to simplify your life so you have less to maintain, insure, clean, and repair. Make a habit of asking yourself whether there's an easier way. Much of our anger is directed at those things that were supposed to make us feel prosperous and happy (e.g., house, car, boat, printer).

Loving, supportive others. Cultivate a network of family, friends, and colleagues who are supportive and loving. Exchanging a good hug can defuse what ticks you off.

Laugh. Finding humor in what ticks you off can help dissipate your anger. If you have fantasies of revenge, make them into an absurd cartoon so you end up laughing.

Turn it into art. Anger over losses, hurts, and betrayals has always been the fodder for literature and art. Journaling about your anger might provide you with a beginning seed for a poem or the plot of a novel. The characters in your life who are irritating or difficult to endure can be transformed into ogres and monsters in a story, or you can write about bad things happening to them.

Self-talk. Notice what you say to yourself. If you start talking more kindly to yourself, you will be less ticked off at others. Since what you say to yourself determines your emotional reaction, you can choose to say something different to yourself to cool off or defuse your anger.

Some suggestions:
This anger is wasting too much of my energy.
I can just listen. I don't have to agree.
I don't have to understand, but I can try.
This will pass.
They don't know better.
I don't have to accept someone else's definition of me.
They don't have the skills to express themselves more appropriately.
It's just a bad day for them (or for me).
I'll go do something productive instead of being angry (e.g., clean, cook, work in the garden, exercise, write an essay).
If I lose my temper, I'll set a bad example for my children (students, employees).
Maybe I misunderstood what they meant.
I'm just wishing this person was different.
This has nothing to do with me.
It's not important enough to get angry about.
Getting angry will only upset me more.
If I say anything while I'm so angry, I'll be sorry later.
I can let this go.
I can choose to interpret this differently.

!

1. How do you nurture yourself? List at least three methods that have worked for you in the past.

   # Next to each item, write when you think you last used this method. If it has been a long time, what keeps you from doing what works?

2. What are your favorite stress busters (e.g., taking a bath, making a cup of herbal tea, listening to music, watching sports, biking)?

3. What exercise do you do to raise your level of serenity (e.g., meditating, walking, practicing yoga, going to the gym)?

4. What can you do to simplify your life? (I stopped wearing makeup and have no clothing that needs to be ironed.) Make a list and then choose one thing you can do (or not do) tomorrow.

5. Who are the people in your loving support network? Write about at least two.

6. If you can't think of two people who are supportive, what first steps can you take to cultivate that kind of friendship? Make a commitment on paper here to do something to invite people into your life.

7. How do you use humor to defuse your anger? List three ways that work for you. (I make a joke inside my head; I tell a joke out loud; I imagine the person naked.)

8. What art can you make to incorporate and resolve your anger (e.g., poetry, drawing, stories, memoir, dance)? Choose something simple/small/short as a start.

9. Who is your role model for transforming anger into art? Write that person's name. How might this person coach you to do the same?

Prompts

10. Who is your role model for dealing with anger? Ask this person what goes on in his or her mind.

11. What self-talk do you use to calm yourself when you are angry? After reading this chapter, what else might you say to yourself?

12. How do you know when your anger is resolved?

>><<

*It is always easier to
fight for one's principles
than to live up to them.*

Alfred Adler

!

Let not the sun go down upon your wrath.

Ephesians 4:26

Many people lose their tempers merely from seeing you keep yours.

Frank Moore Colby

\# ! @!*#@!!#**@#!#*!..........

Conclusion

Getting angry is part of being human. Our angry feelings are signals that tell us to make a change—in our circumstances or in the way we interpret our circumstances. We always have a choice about what to do with our anger. We can be prepared with strategies to defuse our anger and to arrive at a different perspective about what makes us angry. We can steer clear of people who provoke us with unreasonable criticism and demands. Taking care of ourselves and setting boundaries can help to approach what ticks us off with humor, compassion, and clear understanding that this moment will pass. It's all small stuff in the realm of the cosmos.

Adams, Kathleen. *Journal to the Self: 22 Paths to Personal Growth.* New York: Warner, 1990.

Bergman, Ronald. *Emotional Fitness Conditioning.* New York: Perigee, 1998.

Bly, Robert. *A Little Book on the Human Shadow.* HarperSanFrancisco, 1988.

Borysenko, Joan. *Minding the Body, Mending the Mind.* New York: Bantam, 1988.

Butler, C.T. Lawrence, and Amy Rothstein. *On Conflict & Consensus.* Food Not Bombs Publishing, 1987.

Cameron, Julia. *The Artist's Way: A Spiritual Path to Higher Creativity.* Los Angeles: Jeremy P. Tarcher/Perigee, 1992

Carlson, Richard. *Don't Sweat the Small Stuff.* New York: Hyperion, 1997.

Covey, Stephen R. *The 7 Habits of Highly Effective People.* New York: Simon & Schuster, 1989.

Crowe, Sandra. *Since Strangling Isn't an Option.* New York: Perigee, 1999.

DeFoore, Bill. *Anger: Deal with It, Heal with It, Stop It from Killing You.* Deerfield Beach, FL: Health Communications, 1991.

Evans, Patricia. *The Verbally Abusive Relationship: How to Recognize It and How to Respond.* Holdbrook, MA: Bob Adams Inc, 1992.

Forward, Susan, with Craig Buck. *Toxic Parents: Overcoming Their Hurtful Legacy and Reclaiming Your Life.* New York: Bantam, 1989.

Goleman, Daniel. *Emotional Intelligence.* New York: Bantam, 1995.

Hendricks, Gay and Kathlyn. *Conscious Loving: The Journey to Co-Commitment.* New York: Bantam, 1990.

Hendrix, Harville. *Getting the Love You Want: A Guide for Couples.* New York: HarperPerennial, 1988.

Johnson, Robert A. *Owning Your Own Shadow: Understanding the Dark Side of the Psyche.* HarperSanFrancisco, 1991.

Kaner, Sam, Lenny Lind, Catherine Toldi, Sarah Fisk, and Duane Berger. *Facilitator's Guide to Participatory Decision-Making.* Philadelphia: New Society, 1996.

Kurtz, Ernest, and Katherine Ketcham. *The Spirituality of Imperfection.* New York: Bantam, 1992.

LeDoux, Joseph. *The Emotional Brain: The Mysterious Underpinnings of Emotional Life.* New York: Simon & Schuster, 1996.

Lee, John, with Bill Stott. *Facing the Fire: Experiencing and Expressing Anger Appropriately.* New York: Bantam, 1993.

Lerner, Harriet. *The Dance of Anger.* New York: HarperPerrenial, 1986.

160

Mazza, Joan. *Dreaming Your Real Self: A Personal Approach to Dream Interpretation.* New York: Perigee, 1998.

___. *Dream Back Your Life: Taking Dream Messages into Life Action—A Practical Guide to Dreams, Daydreams, and Fantasies.* New York: Perigee, 2000.

___. *From Dreams to Discovery.* Cincinnati: Writer's Digest, 2001.

Pennebaker, James. *Opening Up: The Healing Power of Expressing Emotions.* New York: Guilford, 1997.

Perry, Susan K. *Writing In Flow: Keys to Enhanced Creativity.* Cincinnati: Writer's Digest, 1999.

Phelps, Stanlee, and Nancy Austin. *The Assertive Woman.* San Luis Obispo, CA: Impact Publishers, 1997.

Pryor, Karen. *Don't Shoot the Dog! The New Art of Teaching and Training.* New York: Bantam, 1984.

Ratey, John, and Catherine Johnson. *Shadow Syndromes: The Mild Forms of Major Mental Disorders That Sabotage Us.* New York: Pantheon, 1997.

Rosenberg, Marshall. *Nonviolent Communication: A Language of Compassion.* Del Mar, CA: PuddleDancer, 1999.

Seligman, Martin E.P. *Learned Optimism: How to Change Your Mind and Your Life.* New York: Pocket, 1991.

___. *What You Can Change... and What You Can't.* New York: Knopf, 1994.

Smith, Manuel. *When I Say No, I Feel Guilty.* New York: Dial Press, 1975.

St. James, Elaine. *Simplify Your Life.* New York: Hyperion, 1994.

Tavris, Carol. *Anger: The Misunderstood Emotion.* New York: Simon & Schuster, 1989.

Weiner-Davis, Michele. *Change Your Life and Everyone in It.* New York: Fireside, 1995.

Whitfield, Charles. *Boundaries and Relationships.* Deerfield Beach, CA: Health Communications, 1993.

Williams, Redford, and Virginia Williams. *Anger Kills.* New York: HarperPerennial, 1993.

Wright, Robert. *The Moral Animal: Why We Are the Way We Are—Evolutionary Psychology.* New York: Vintage, 1994.

Zweig, Connie, and Jeremiah Abrams (editors). *Meeting the Shadow: The Hidden Power of the Dark Side of Human Nature.* Los Angeles: Jeremy P. Tarcher, 1991.

___. *Romancing the Shadow: Illuminating the Dark Side of the Soul.* New York: Ballantine, 1997.